CW00429510

...stuff Ben said
Volume 1

GEORGE CHUTER
AND TOM CROFT

Published in the United Kingdom by We R Publishing Ltd in 2015.

Copyright © We R Publishing Ltd, 2015.
All rights reserved.

George Chuter and Tom Croft have asserted their right under the Copyright, Designs and Patents Act, 1988 to be identified as the author of this work.

This book is sold subject to the condition that it shall not, by way of trade or otherwise, be lent, resold, hired out, or otherwise circulated without the publisher's prior consent in any form of binding or cover other than which it is published and without a simiilar condition, including this condition, being imposed on the subsequent purchaser.

First edition published in the United Kingdom in 2015 by We R Publishing Ltd.

We R Publishing Ltd
Beechtrees | Church Lane | Newton | Wisbech
Cambridgeshire | PE13 5HF | United Kingdom

We R Publishing Ltd Reg. No. 08013823.

A CIP catalogue record for this book is available from the British Library.

ISBN 978-0-9932952-0-1

We R Publishing Ltd is committed to a sustainable future for our business, our readers and our planet. This book is made from paper certified by the Forest Stewardship Council.

Edited by: George Chuter and Tom Croft.
Illustration by: Patrick Latham.
Font: Cronos Pro.
Printed & bound in the UK by John Baxter & Sons Limited
Hinckley, Leicestershire, LE10 1YG.

...stuff Ben said
Volume 1

WRITTEN AND EDITED BY
George Chuter and Tom Croft

COVER DESIGN
Patrick Latham

PUBLISHED BY
We R Publishing Ltd

SUPPORTING
Matt Hampson Foundation

...stuff Ben said

Please note this is a book published from the Twitter feed @stuffbensaid - based on the life of Leicester Tigers, England and British and Irish Lion, Ben Youngs.

He goes by many names, which are listed below for your information whilst reading this book.

• BEN
• LEN
• LENNY
• LENDRID

This book was launched on his wedding day as a surprise to Ben. Who knew he'd publish his own book and get married on the same day......clever boy!!!!

Norfolk meaning North Folk is England's most eastern county. A hot spot for British holidaymakers, bird watchers and city slickers looking for that retreat away from the hustle and bustle of London life.

Its idyllic coastline running for 100 miles not only caters for the thriving tourist trade but is also the 'office' for many a fisherman.

Lord Nelson born here in 1758, paved the way with his victory in Trafalgar for numerous successes to emerge over the coming centuries, I'd like to introduce to you one of these native Norfolkians, Ben Youngs.

This anthology of comments, thoughts and remarks, first started in 2010 in Australia whilst on tour with England Rugby. One evening, whilst on a team meal out, the food was ordered and the platters were delivered to the table. Mounds of fresh seafood spread out before us and the boys tucked in. Ben, tucking into his favourite calamari, accidentally strayed across the platter border and scooped up a muscle with his aioli covered fingers. Not knowing what he had discovered, he prized the muscle open and devoured.

"Wow that was nice, I don't think I've ever had oysters before"......and at this point @stuffbensaid was born.

Over the next 5 years, George Chuter, Tom Croft and a network of spies spread across the country, including his own family relayed his pearls of wisdom that came from this very special boys mind - and instantaneously were documented in his dedicated Twitter feed @stuffbensaid.

This book gives you further insight to these comments and also the thoughts and opinions of some of the greatest rugby players and sportsmen from across the world on Ben Youngs.

So, whether your reclining on the sofa or sat on the toilet in the sanctity of your bathroom, enjoy these pearls of wisdom and let your mind wonder as I present to you...

...@stuffbensaid

...stuff Ben said

It gives me great pleasure to write a foreword in a book that shows that backs can say as many stupid things as forwards.

On the field, Ben is as sharp as a tack, off it, as demonstrated by this book - not so much.

As a huge fan of sports statistics, I ran the numbers through Opta, and the results were astonishing.

On average, Lenny speaks 1247 times per day.

1.29% of the time, he is talking about food.

1.98% of the time, he is talking about his PlayStation.

This leaves a whopping 96.73% of his speech dedicated to the type of stuff that's in this book. I expect this means that there will be a new version released every year from now on.

Congratulations on the marriage, and I hope you managed to free up a couple of percent on your wedding day, to talk about your new wife.

Best wishes.

Martin Johnson

Leicester Tigers, England and British & Irish Lion Captain.

Volume 1

"What's that island with all the stone heads on it? Isn't it called Easter Egg Island?"

(Ben deciding where he wanted to go on holiday.)

....

"Right! I'm on a diet. I'm gonna eat nothing but juice tomorrow."

....

"I'm 25 and my kid is 4 months old. When I'm 90 he'll be about 50 and we can go to Necker Island together. I'm saving up already."

(After watching the documentary on Richard Branson.)

....

"Grapefruit? It's disgusting. Who invented this shit??"

"I buy myself presents and write 'To Ben, from Lendrid' on them. Then I try to forget what I bought so I can surprise myself."

(Before Christmas every year.)

....

Tom: *"We saw a midwife today. She said it will be a while yet."*
Lendrid: *"Will the Mrs be diluted?"*
Tom: *"Do you mean induced?"*
Lendrid: *"Oh yeah."*

....

Lendrid: *"What are they mum?"*
Mum: *"Courgette fries."*
Lendrid: *"What, as in courgette fish?"*
Mum: *"No, as in courgette vegetables darling."*

I cannot begin to tell you the pleasure compiling @stuffbensaid has given me over the last 5 years.

Whenever I receive a text informing me of yet another idiotic comment, the feeling I get when opening it is just like the feeling I get when opening a Christmas present, or a new bottle of Jim Beam.

Lenny has been a great bud, and we could have potentially been best buds, had he been 10 years older and me 5 years younger. I feel I owe him a huge debt of gratitude for providing me with an endless supply of after-dinner speaking material.

The sign of a great story is that, when you tell it, the audience actually thinks you are telling a joke when in fact; you are simply informing them of something Lenny said the other day. Pure genius.

It is a huge honour for me to write an entry in this great book. I feel it could change the face of literature as we know it, and I am very proud to have been there on the ground floor when this change began.

Oh. Best bud, heres to another 20 years of laughs.

George Chuter

Leicester Tigers and England.

Lendrid: *"I hated that abscess short."*
Tom: *"It's called absinth."*

(On a night out.)

....

Lendrid: *"You know those Charlie's
we fought in the war?"*
Tom: *"Charlie's??"*
Lendrid: *"Yeah, you know? The Germans?"*
Tom: *"They were called Jerry's."*

....

Me: *"Brian only has one lung, lost the
other to cancer."*
Lendrid: *"I only found out we had two
lungs last year. Can't remember how
I found out."*

....

"Oh. I'd love a can of John Smith's tuna right now."

Lendrid: *"I think I'm having permutations."*
Tom: *"Huh?"*
Lendrid: *"My heart is beating really weirdly."*
Tom: *"Thats called palpitations."*

....

Lendrid: *"Bomage!"*
Tom: *"Huh?"*
Lendrid: *"Bomage! It's French for Goodbye."*

....

Lendrid: *"I'm a great heckler, me."*
Tom: *"Heckler?"*
Lendrid: *"Yeah you know, I can get the prices down really well."*
Tom: *"That's haggling."*

....

Lendrid: *"So why is it called 'Return of the King'?"*

Tom: *"Because Aragorn returns to be king."*
Lendrid: *"Aragorn is the king? I never knew that."*

....

Lendrid: *"Can't wait to buy my kid salvation family."*
Tom: *"Huh?"*
Lendrid: *"Oh yeah, not salvation, Slovenian family."*
Tom: *"It's Sylvanian family."*

....

I'm Spain-Went in restraint said do you do creps they say no.Say follow me take me to another restraint.Point to some crabs. What do I do?

(The text I received from Ben whilst he was holidaying in Spain with his wife.)

I have to say that I'm a big fan of Ben's. He is a fantastic bloke, a phenomenal player and an immense rugby nause. I loved my time playing alongside him in an England shirt and even opposite him in a Toulon one. He embodies humility and respect.

My favourite example of his very humble side was during the RWC 2011 when he did a nice piece with the Times newspaper, going through the squad and ripping the piss out of each player. He made everyone out to be this tight group of best mates recounting their tomfoolery and hilarious horseplay. Each team member had a nice little story about them in there too.

When it came to describing me, so keen was he not to offend, and so respectful (weak) was the quote and so phenomenally boring (weak) was story, that in the end the whole article portrayed me to be, by quite a margin, the dullest, dourest and most unlikeable member of the team. Which to be fair wasn't a million miles off - but that's not the point.

To be thought of in such a way by such an incredible talent though, a talent for making without doubt some of the weirdest and most disturbing comments ever heard (as seen @stuffbensaid) will easily do for me.

Good luck to you mate, you are a top bloke and your world is at your feet as you deserve it to be. Embrace it.

Jonny Wilkinson

England and British and Irish Lions.

A plate of biscuits comes out -
Lendrid: *"Oh. Look how nice they look with all that flour over them."*
Tom: *"Thats icing sugar."*

....

Lendrid: "George Foreman has six sons all called George!"
Tom: "The boxer? That's mad."
Lendrid: "No not the boxer. The bloke who makes the grills."

....

Being introduced for a Q&A alongside Flood and Croft -
MC: *"And born in Norfolk, I'd like to introduce..."*
Lendrid: *"Oh! That might be me."*

(Flood born in Surrey, Croft in Hampshire.)

Never have I heard such nonsense come from
the mouth of someone so capable of speaking
so much sense.

Lenny maybe a slightly more intelligent version of
Julian Salvi but he never ceases to make me smile
with his gibberish.

I was out with Crofty when Lenny called up, he
starts explaining to Len how to make his Irish
stew, step by step he talks him through it,
down to the finest detail.

- chop the onions - yes peel them first,
- brown the lamb - yes in a hot pan,
- cover everything in stock!

15 minutes later Crofty gets another call from what
sounds like a panicking Lenny. He goes through it
again step by step finishing with the stock.

Crofty pauses to think, then asks if Len has added
water to the stock?

There lay the problem, GENIUS!!!!!

Matthew Tait

Leicester Tigers and England.

*"He was the top shagger on tour.
He won the Gold T-Shirt."*

....

"Ah, America. Home of the land."

(Land of the Free, Home of the Brave - almost there!)

....

In the words of the great actor Liam
Nelson, *"I will find you, and I will kill you."*

(Whilst talking about the blockbuster 'Taken', starring
Liam Neeson!)

....

Lendrid: *"If you could invent anything
that's been invented, what would it be?"*
Julian: *"Google. How about you?"*
Lendrid: *"Oil."*

Lendrid: *"When's your wedding?"*
Blaine: *"July 4th."*
Lendrid: *"Oh! Happy New Year!"*
Blaine: *"I think you mean Happy Independence Day."*
Lendrid: *"Oh."*

....

Lendrid: *"They produce athletes like they come off a treadmill."*
Ryan: *"Don't you mean a conveyor belt?"*
Lendrid: *"Oh yeah."*

....

"Oh! He's plucked that ball out of the air like a child."

Tom: *"How much was that? £40?"*
Lendrid: *"No way! It wasn't that much!!
It was £39.99."*

....

*"Wow! Arsenal lost 6-3! You really get money
for your value there!"*

....

"That was like Moses departing the Red Sea."

....

"I split it like an axe."

(In the physio room, after getting a cut in training.)

....

"I think he's mugging me on."

Lady: *"This photo-shoot might run a bit late tonight. Is that ok?"*
Lendrid: *"Yes no problem. I'm a night bird anyway."*

....

Lendrid: *"We can go to Vegas and stay in a pension!"*
Tom: *"Huh?"*
Lendrid: *"You know, a room at the top of the hotel."*
Tom: *"It's called a penthouse"*

....

Lendrid: *"What date is the Friday?"*
Tom: *"The 29th."*
Lendrid: *"So what day is the 30th?"*

....

"I want to learn sign language so I can speak it."

I love it, its funny, every time we'll be chatting in the changing room Lenny will come out with something completely out the blue, and the lads will look at him and think f**king hell Len!

Manu Tuilagi

Leicester Tigers, England and British and Irish Lions.

....

He's world class both on and off the field, the catalyst for a lot of Leicester and England's attacking prowess.

However, he's also the catalyst for the majority of the entertainment off the field too, unknowingly!

@stuffbensaid is an unbelievably true account and window into the mind of this special player and friend.

Chris Robshaw

Harlequins and Captain of England.

Lendrid: *"I love the bloke's voice in 'Robin Hood Prince of Thieves' when he shouts 'Huxley! Huxley!'"*
Tom: *"It's Locksley."*

···

"Mike Phillips played really well on tour, and obviously he started 2 out of the first one tests."

(After the 2013 Lions tour to South Africa.)

···

Lendrid: *"I'm having a peanut butter sandwich with non-toasted bread."*
Dan: *"Bread then..."*

···

Lendrid naming places in Africa -
"Kenya, Tanzania, Bonsiorna."

"Watched a new film today - Escape from Albatross."

. . . .

Lendrid: *"Right, let me get this right. Olive trees don't grow olives do they?"*
Tom: *"Yes they do."*
Lendrid: *"No seriously, what do they grow on?"*

. . . .

"Wow! I feel like Troy in Brad Pitt."

(After doing an upper-body weights session.)

. . . .

"I could be like a cat. You know, with those 8 lives they have. Or 9. However many it is."

Ben Youngs is the lad that every rugby team needs the guy who cracks the jokes at the most inappropriate times, and gets away with it. His attitude to life and rugby is simple, be happy - and it is contagious.

One of my favourite players to have played along side, he could change a game in an instant and always find a way to enjoy himself and his teammates company.

Born and breed in Norfolk and molded in the fires of Leicester being a small part of his success as a person gives me great pride.

I know if he had his way I'd be coaching him at Tigers, and no doubt he'd be my Captain. Lenny don't change, the game needs men like you.

Now... Before I finish, I must say Lenny is also one of the stupidest people I know, he once asked me after reading the back page of a newspaper why people die in alphabetical order! And on a pre-season trip to France couldn't understand why the guy who swam the English Channel and got tired at halfway and turned around and swam back was a joke.

BFF Newbs.

Craig Newby

Leicester Tigers and New Zealand All Black.

Lendrid doing some quick arithmetic whilst arranging a dinner party -

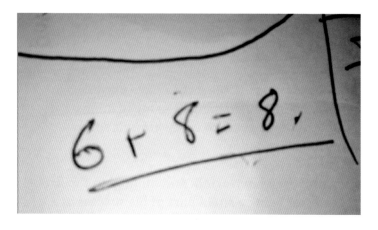

....

Sue Barker: *"Ben, a true or false question now - Goran Ivanesevic lost to Tim Henman in the semi-final of Wimbledon. True or false?"*
Lendrid: *"Wrong."*

(During his 1st appearance on A Question of Sport.)

....

"I'm not stupid. I just don't always know the pacific words."

The most miraculous thing about Lenny and his funny little life isn't that he has been so successful in rugby. No, it's that he has managed, despite his clear and obvious flaws, to make his way in the big wide world.

He has a proper job a house and even a car. For someone born with negative amounts of common sense, no obvious knowledge of what is actually going on around him, and zero ability to assess any given situation in which height find himself, he is doing incredibly well, the special little soldier.

His handlers must be proud.

David Flatman

Bath and England.

....

Good bugger. Deadly with ball in hand, won't stop yapping like a Jack Russell with his nuts caught in a rat trap.

Tony Woodcock

New Zealand All Black (110 caps).

Ryan Lamb is practicing goal kicking and nails one -
Lendrid: *"Nice one Lamby! You just bicepted the posts!"*

· ·

Me: *"Knock-knock?"*
Lendrid: *"Who's there?"*
Me: *"Atish."*
Lendrid: *"Atish?"*
Me: *"Atish."*
Lendrid: *"Atish? Oh sorry. Atish who? I forgot how the joke went."*

· ·

George: *"Your appointment is on Wednesday 18th September."*
Lendrid: *"Ok. Is that a Wednesday?"*

Being a livestock farmer, I'm used to spending time with somewhat stupid animals. However, reading @stuffbensaid has given me a new appreciation of the intelligence of sheep and cattle. Lenny might be one of the best scrumhalves in rugby, but he would be bottom of the class in my herd of Devonshire's.

It was great playing alongside Ben for a few years, and this book will allow me to relive some of those memories time and time again.

Julian White

Leicester Tigers, England and British and Irish Lions.

....

He's my brother so its tough to be mean to him, and to be honest most of what he says makes a lot of sense to me.

But, every now and then, he says something that just confuses me as to how he's got to that point - because there's just no obvious way to get to that point!

Tom Youngs (brother)

Leicester Tigers, England and British and Irish Lions.

Lendrid: *"You know that prawn shop in Leicester?"*
Tom: *"Prawn shop?"*
Lendrid: *"Yeah you know? That shop where you swap things."*

....

"I didn't do very well at that pub quiz. I couldn't remember the answers."

....

Lendrid: *"Israel Folou flies like the raspberry flop!"*
Tom: *"Don't you mean Fosbury Flop?"*
Lendrid: *"No. I know what I mean - it's a high jump technique."*

(After the first test in Australia during the 2013 Lions.)

Dan: *"What's the name of the old guy in 'The Karate Kid'?"*
Lendrid: *"I think its Mr. Mugabe."*

....

"You know when the world was all connected, well when it all broke up, where did all the extra water come from?"

(In Sydney Harbour discussing Pangea with Ben.)

....

"My fact of the day is that the Channel Tunnel goes under the sea."

....

"Oh! I felt like Neil Armstrong climbing the Moon!"

(After climbing the Sydney Harbour Bridge.)

Lendrid: *"My favourite song by 'The Who' is 'Piano Wizard'. I love it!"*
Tom: *"You mean 'Pinball Wizard?"*
Lendrid: *"Oh, yeah..."*

· ·

Lendrid: *"Ugh! I hate rum. It's disgusting. What's that you're drinking?"*
Tom: *"A mojito."*
Lendrid: *"Ooohhh! I love them!"*

· ·

Lendrid: *"You know those sticks that burn incense?"*
Tom: *"You mean incense sticks?"*
Lendrid: *"Yeah, those ones."*

Lendrid: *"Would you use euthanasia on your pet if you had to?"*
Tom: *"You mean have them put down?"*
Lendrid: *"Yeah, that too."*

....

Ben: *"For this advert, you've got to squash yellow things."*
Lendrid: *"Like bananas and lemons? Knowing me, I'll probably lime myself in the eye!"*

(During filming for the 2013 Lions media campaign.)

....

Lendrid: *"These jeans have a shoe horn on."*
Tom: *"Huh?"*
Lendrid: *"One of those things horses have on their feet to stop their nails breaking."*
Tom: *"Horse shoe?"*

Tom: *"This place has all the shops!"*
Lendrid: *"Does it have American Express?"*
Tom: *"Huh?"*
Lendrid: *"You know. The American Express shop!"*

....

What a top lad, was a pleasure to get to know him on the Lions Tour in 2013, however it left me a little uncertain in retrospect about some of the conversations we had.

All until reading @stuffbensaid.

Now it's clear looking back that what he said was, what he actually said, and not something I misheard, this book reassures me as well as entertains!

Coming from a farming background, obviously I was amazed to hear that when asked what the main ingredient in Weetabix was, he said barley - truly genius.

Dan Lydiate

Opsreys, Wales and British and Irish Lions.

Lendrid: *"Can I have some of that butter please?"*
Graham: *"It's egg yolk."*

....

Tom: *"Why shouldn't I do woodwork?"*
Lendrid: *"Two reasons - 1, you're shit and 3, it'll fall apart."*
Tom: *"What happened to number 2?"*
Lendrid: *"Oh."*

....

Lendrid: *"San Marino are 100/1 to win. I'm going to put £10 on them. I could win £100,000!"*
Tom: *"That's not right!"*
Lendrid: *"Oh. £10,000 then."*

"I'm so bored of having chicken for dinner. Anyone fancy going to Nandos?"

....

Lendrid: *"I want one of those blind dogs."*
Toby: *"Blind dogs?"*
Lendrid: *"You know, those blind dogs."*
Toby: *"You mean guide dog?"*
Lendrid: *"Oh yeah."*

....

Nick: *"What's barley used for?"*
Lendrid: *"Weetabix?"*
Nick: *"What's wheat used for then?"*
Lendrid: *"Beer?"*

(Talking to his dad Nick, owner of one of the largest farms in Norfolk.)

....

"I love all the Christmas cheeses. Cheddar, Stilton, Camenbrie."

Lendrid: *"I wonder who invented basketball?"*
George: *"It was a bloke called Dr. Tim Basketball."*
Lendrid: *"Really? Wow! That's amazing!"*

....

Working with Lenny as a rugby player is a pleasure, his hard work and quick thinking has led to the victories for both Leicester Tigers and for England.

What I fail to work out still is how such a quick decisive thinker on the pitch can quickly think so little off the pitch - in real life!

Some of the things this kid comes out with can only be described as bizarre and has left not only myself but countless others in complete amazement!

Graham Rowntree

Leicester Tigers, England and British and Irish Lions.

Lendrid: *"My favourite film is on later!"*
Tom: *"What film is that?"*
Lendrid: *"Breadsticks and Broomknobs."*
Tom: *"It's Bedknobs and Broomsticks."*

....

Tom: *"Lenny, name something that is traditionally eaten at Easter."*
Lendrid: *"Bunny?"*

(Playing a Christmas quiz.)

....

Lendrid: *"My stew is really dry."*
Tom: *"Did you add stock?"*
Lendrid: *"Yes 2 cubes."*
Tom: *"Did you add water to the cubes?"*
Lendrid: *"Do I need to?"*

Having been a man of limited IQ myself I find it very easy to spot those total idiots that share a similar level of intelligence. With the complete in ability to dis-engage the mouth before the flow of perceived intelligent information spills forth. Lenny welcome to my world!!

I have read with huge enjoyment the @stuffbensaid over the years it is a daily source of moral boosting joy for me and it makes me wonder how Lenny has survived for so long on this planet!!

Now the above statements might seem harsh but I see it quite differently. As ben is one of those loyal and commuted characters that life would quite frankly be boring without. He is Someone who doesn't take him self to seriously has a very simple outlook on life and gives the rest of us when around him a great deal of enjoyment.

Lenny, have a great wedding day enjoy the next chapter of your life as a married man. Most importantly don't ever stop being my friend, you continually brighten up our lives and make this world an enjoyable place.

Love to you both on this very special day.

Moodos

Lewis Moody

Leicester Tigers, England and British and Irish Lions.

Lendrid: *"Those glasses make you look like Cark Klent!"*
George: *"Who?!"*
Lendrid: *"You know! Superman!"*

....

Tom: *"Do you want some mulled wine, Lendrid?"*
Lendrid: *"Yes, but it's not Halloween is it?"*

....

"I think this juicer is broken. I've put a load of nuts in and nothing is coming out."

....

"Blueberries are really good for you, aren't they? They're full of anti-oxygen's."

Owen: *"I've got a really bunged up nose."*
Lendrid: *"You want to get some volvic for that."*
Owen: *"Do you mean Vicks?"*

....

Giulia: *"I'm really struggling with my English lessons. I have trouble remembering the verbs."*
Lendrid: *"I know them. A-E-I-O-U."*

....

Lendrid: *"Got a great bargain for flights to New York!"*
Dan: *"Doesn't look that good a bargain"*
Lendrid: *"Yeah, well its cheaper than if I drove."*

"We should dress real English in New York. You know, chinos, shirt, wafers."

(During a mid season trip to New York.)

....

I first met Lenny at Tigers and he was the most welcoming guy at the club, he helped me settle in when I was coming into the 1st team, which I will always be grateful for.

He's a great lad to be around, always upbeat and having a laugh, and an even better rugby player to play along side.

Some of the things he comes out with are priceless and he genuinely believes what he has said is not stupid.

The classic one I heard was when travelling with England away to Ireland. Arriving at the airport in Ireland and getting on the coach, Len turned around and asked how the coach got here before us!

No better 9 on or off the field!

George Ford
Bath and England.

Lendrid: *"You can't freeze milk, can you?"*
Tom: *"Yeah of course you can."*
Lendrid: *"No you can't. It'll go off."*

....

Lendrid: *"God! I love this song!"*
Tom: *"What's it called?"*
Lendrid: *"Benny And The Jerry's."*

(Listening to 'Bennie And The Jets' by Elton John.)

....

Coming into land at the airport -
Lendrid: *"Wow! Are those traffic jams down there?"*
Tom: *"No Lenny. They're street lights."*

Lendrid: *"So what's in horseradish sauce then?"*
Charlie: *"Er, horseradish!"*
Lendrid: *"Yeah, but what's in it?"*

....

"I've just got back from Greece. Food was great. Loads of veal. I thought that was weird though because I didn't see any Deer around."

....

"Our chiropractor against their chiropractor is a rivalry like the Montague's against the Capricorns in Romeo and Juliette."

....

"Are Danny De Vito and Arnold Swartzenegger really twins?"

Woman at airport check-in: *"Does anyone here have a surname from the beginning of the alphabet?"*
Ben: (with his hand up) *"Yes, I do."*

....

Tom: *"Have you got your fancy dress yet?"*
Lendrid: *"Yes. It's nothing special. It's just made of pylon."*

....

Lendrid: *"What are all those white things floating around?"*
Tom: *"They're clouds Lenny."*

(Watching a documentary on Earth from space.)

Charlie: *"What religion was your school?"*
Lendrid*:* *"Ummm...Duke of Edinburgh."*
Charlie: *"Do you mean Church of England?"*
Lendrid: *"Yeah that's it."*

....

In Rome -
Tom: *"Lenny, you fancy going to see the Coliseum and the Leaning Tower of Pisa tomorrow?"*
Lendrid: *"Yeah can do."*

....

Matt: *"How was the Calcutta Cup made?"*
Lendrid: *"It was made from a melted-down Indian ruby."*

"I don't get it. Why are there elephants and stuff on the Calcutta Cup? What's it got to do with India?"

(After winning the Calcutta Cup in 2011.)

....

Lendrid: *"Wow! Look at that! I love Maserati's!"*
Tom: *"That's a Jaguar."*

....

"There were supposed to be 8 of us doing the coaching tomorrow but to make it easier on the boys we've doubled up. So now there are 18 of us."

Tom: *"So Lendrid, which British athletes are you most looking forward to seeing at the Olympics?"*
Lendrid: *"Erm, probably Usain Bolt."*

(Before heading of to watch the London Olympics.)

∙∙

Charlie: *"Lendrid, I asked for a pastry brush. That's a tip-ex brush!"*
Lendrid: *"I know. Can't you just wash it off and use it?"*

(After being sent to the supermarket to get ingredients, mixing bowl and pastry brush.)

∙∙

Tom: *"Warhorse was an awesome film. It's a true story as well."*
Lendrid: *"I know. It was written by the horse."*

Lendrid: *"I love snakes and lizards. All those erotic pets are brilliant."*
Ben: *"I think you mean exotic."*

··

"Where's Hampshire? Sounds like it's miles away."

··

Lendrid: *"You should be CEO of @stuffbensaid."*
George: *"What does CEO mean then?"*
Lendrid: *"Er, I don't know."*

··

"Come on everyone. Lets do the New Year countdown again! 10...9...7...6...5..."

"I love my new coffee machine. Where do I get those Nesquik pods from though?"

....

Lendrid: *"Mmm, this soup is really hydrating me."*
Tom: *"That's porridge Lenny."*

(During pre match meal.)

....

Tom: *"I can't believe petrol is £1.40 and diesel is £1.43."*
Lendrid: *"I know! Why is diesel £3 more expensive?"*

My favourite Lenny story was when he was recovering from knee surgery & I asked him *"how was the range"* to which Ben replied *"Oh Matty I've never experienced anything like it."* So I repeated the question *"how is the range"* and again he said *"amazing ride, I've never driven anything like it, do you want to take it for a spin".*

Ben was referring to the recently collected RANGE ROVER SPORT that was one of the benefits of being selected for England and not his recently operated on knee.

Ben was a pleasure to coach - he was a great guy, even as a very young player for bringing the best out of others. He always enjoyed the environment and that was contagious.

As a player there is no better 9 at challenging defenders but still providing space and opportunities for his runners.

Matt O'Connor

Australia and Curent Head Coach of Leinster.

Lendrid: *"I love that Christmas song by Sledge. I mean Sleigh."*
George: *"It's Slade."*

....

"We've got to start what we've finished."

(During a half time speech whilst playing Wasps at home.)

....

"She used to be horrendously ugly when she was younger, but now she's gorgeous. She's turned from a duck into a swan."

....

Lendrid: *"Had to see a pediatrician today."*
Charlie: *"What?! Why?"*
Lendrid: *"Got my feet checked and nails trimmed."*
Charlie: *"That's a podiatrist."*

Lendrid: *"I love TOWNIE"*
Charlie: *"What's TOWNIE?"*
Lendrid: *"The Only Way Is Essex silly!"*
Charlie: *"I think you mean TOWIE."*

....

"My parents are flying to New Zealand via Dubai. That means they'll arrive here yesterday doesn't it?"

....

Lendrid in a restaurant: *"What's a blat sandwich?"*
Dan: *"That says BLT."*

....

Toby: *"If NZ has Christmas in the summer, does that mean it's in August there?"*
Lendrid: *"No you idiot. Obviously it's in November like us."*

Tom: *"I've just been sailing in America's Cup sail boats around the Tasman Sea."*
Lendrid: *"Why aren't they in America then?"*

....

Lendrid: *"You know those sky-scrapers of houses?"*
Tom: *"You mean a block of flats?"*
Lendrid: *"Yeah whatever it's called."*

....

Waitress: *"Can I take your order sir?"*
Lendrid: *"Umm...yes. Can I have the fish and chips please, with a side order of chips?"*

I used to listen to Lenny talk, and I would think, "Is he for real?"

I resisted the urge to bang him out for being stupid, and eventually found out that he was being pretty funny. When I found out he wasn't being funny deliberately, I about dropped the tea bags I was carrying! I couldn't believe someone could be that daft.

Lenny has been a good mate and teammate for a while now, but I still don't know how he gets out of the house every day, let alone remembers to get dressed, and breathe all the time.

Fortunately, he's now got a good wife to help him do all the important stuff. As long as he remembers his lines on the wedding day!

It's been a privilege following @stuffbensaid, and contributing to this book.

Congratulations mate. All the best.

Louis Deacon

Leicester Tigers and England.

Petrol station tannoy: *"Can the man at pump 12 please move. That's an HGV pump."*
Lendrid (at pump 12): *"Oh. I thought the hose was a bit big."*

....

Ben: *"Surely a battered mars bar will melt when cooked."*
Tom: *"It's battered before frying."*
Ben: *"What?! Why would you put batter on a mars bar."*

....

"I haven't tweeted for 20 days! That's nearly 2 weeks."

....

"I didn't realise killer whales were nasty."

(Watching a David Attenborough wildlife documentary about the sea.)

Tom: *"I wonder if Susan Ma is on Facebook?"*
Lendrid: *"No idea. I don't know how to spell her second name."*

(Watching The Apprentice.)

....

Dan: *"Where abouts in Leicester do you live? In town?"*
Lendrid: *"No. I live in the countryside bit."*

....

I have been lucky enough to know Ben for a few years now and even more privileged to play with him. Rugby is running short of characters and luckily Ben is one of the last ones going. He is a super professional who always sets the standard in anything that he does.

I have always enjoyed playing with him, especially as he always passes me the ball. He has grown as a leader and is becoming a vocal voice of leadership certainly in the England squad, as well a captaining the Tigers.

The Leicester boys are a very tight knit bunch who every rarely leave each other's sides; they are a bit like the Borg from Star Trek. They share one mind and go everywhere together.

Ben however is a bit of renegade; he has broken out that mould and often leaves the group to come mingle with us non-tigers men. He then rushes back to tell the lads what is going on outside the clique. He is their man on the inside you could say, sharing the stories and going ons of the strange outside world.

I was only recently made aware of the twitter site @stuffbensaid. Little did I know that Ben aka Lendrid says such special things! He seems to hide this very well when he is rolling with the non Leicester boys. However one classic that made me laugh was:

Tom: *"My dog is going to have puppies."*
Lendrid: *"Who's the father?"*
Tom: *"A Polish dog."*
Lendrid: *"Oh no! How will they talk to each other?"*

James Haskell

Wasps and England.

Interviewer: *"What's your favourite holiday destination?"*
Lendrid: *"Las Vegas. I've never been though."*

⋯⋯⋯⋯⋯⋯⋯⋯⋯⋯⋯⋯⋯⋯⋯⋯⋯⋯

"Saw an awesome movie last night. Can't remember what it's called. Begins with 's'. Got it! 'Insidious.'"

⋯⋯⋯⋯⋯⋯⋯⋯⋯⋯⋯⋯⋯⋯⋯⋯⋯⋯

"What actually is the difference between these two? My girlfriend asked me to buy them."

(Looking at a corkscrew and a can opener.)

⋯⋯⋯⋯⋯⋯⋯⋯⋯⋯⋯⋯⋯⋯⋯⋯⋯⋯

"I don't get hot air balloons. All you do is sit in a basket surrounded by fire. How is that fun?"

Lendrid: *"You should get your antiques on that TV show 'In Your Closet.'"*
Tom: *"You mean 'Cash In The Attic.'"*
Lendrid: *"Yeah that's the one."*

....

Question: *"Who shares their surname with a German city? Irving Berlin, Paris Hilton or George Washington?"*
Lendrid: *"Washington! Some yokel will say Paris Hilton."*

....

Tom: *"We're having Thai for dinner tonight."*
Lendrid: *"Thai? Awesome! Chingquia! That's Thai for thank you."*
Tom: *"Er, that's Polish."*

"I can't believe they've lit that indoors!"

(After seeing a fake flickering candle in furniture shop.)

....

In an antiques shop -
Lendrid: *"Cor! That's an awesome sundial on the wall over there!"*
Tom: *"That's a clock Lenny."*

....

"I've just viewed a house. It was lovely. It's got beams and it's just been revenerated."

....

News: *"Samoa to lose a day to catch up time with New Zealand."*
Lendrid: *"Why don't they just stay on Friday for a week?"*

Lenny is possibly one of the best rugby players I have ever played with, but could quiet possibly be one of the stupidest players I have played with as well. However, spending most days with him at training he does offer very good entertainment, and keeps the boys laughing with his very unique out look on life.

I love that @stuffbensaid exists so that everyone can experience some of these gems Lenny comes out with.

For those of you who don't know Lenny too well just picture Bruce from Matilda trapped inside a rugby player's body. My favourite @stuffbensaid quote has to be:

Lendrid: *"Why is it called a bank holiday?"*
George: *"Because the banks are shut."*
Lendrid: *"Mine's not. I've just got money out of the cashpoint."*

How can a man that's lived on earth for over 20 years not know one what a bank holiday is and two that a cashpoint works 24/7.

So let's hope for many more laughs from the man-child they call Lenny.

Jordan Crane

Leicester Tigers and England.

Tom: *"I'd love to live in a windmill."*
Lendrid: *"I wouldn't. You'd get dizzy all the time."*

....

"I've just got a 3D TV. The picture is unbelievable, especially when I'm on the PlayStation. I wish life was in 3D."

....

"Would you rather have lived in Roman times, gladiator times or Apocalypse times?"

....

Looking at a map of New Zealand -
"Wow! That's a long beach! Does the coast go all around New Zealand?"

As we board a coach at Dublin Airport -
Lendrid: *"Isn't this the bus we got to East Midlands airport? How did it get here before us?"*
Tom: *"Different coach mate."*

(Different coach, same company!)

···

"I had such a weird dream last night. I dreamt I had a kid and she got adducted."

···

Lendrid: *"I had one of those horror dreams last night."*
Tom: *"You mean a nightmare?"*
Lendrid: *"Yeah it was a right nightmare."*

···

"I'm absolutely starving. I hope there's food at this barbecue."

Some say the quickest route is as the crow flies,
but Lenny proves that this isn't always the case.
For such a talented quick thinking rugby player,
you can physically hear the cogs moving in his
head when you get him thinking outside the box.

Sat in Sydney Harbour drinking coffee and
discussing Pangea, the mass of land which broke
up to form the continents as we know them today,
Ben pauses and then asks the question which only
he could, "Where did the extra water come from to
fill the gaps when the bits of land moved apart?"

Pure gold, although I fear that as he's grown
older he's learnt to hold his tongue - allowing
his mind to catch up. So few and far between his
comments have become, the more excited I now
get when one appears.

Volume 2 who knows!

Tom Croft

Leicester Tigers, England and British and Irish Lions.

Lendrid: *"I've just cooked lamb in a port and redcurrant sauce."*
Tom: *"Nice. What's in the sauce?"*
Lendrid: *"Port and...erm, something else."*

....

Tom: *"How was last night Lendrid?"*
Lendrid: *"One word mate –
F**king Mental!"*

....

News headline: *"Oxford man killed by an arsenal of weapons."*
Me: *"I wonder if he was at Oxford Uni?"*
Lendrid: *"No. It says he was from Arsenal."*

Tom: *"Workers at Alton Towers don't get paid. They collect coins that fall out on upside down rides."*
Lendrid: *"Really? That's a good idea."*

(During trip to Alton Towers and walking beneath the roller coaster.)

....

Tom: *"A man swam exactly halfway across the Channel, then turned back as he was bored."*
Lendrid: *"Idiot! He should have just swam the rest!"*

(An early test to see how Bens mind really worked.)

....

Tom: *"They've started breeding live salmon with cream cheese and chive filling already in it."*
Lendrid: *"Wow! Modern science is so amazing."*

(During the Premiership awards evening 2009, we had salmon roulade for starter.)

Mae un o'r blokes garedicaf yn y byd rygbi
, ac un o'r mwyaf doniol oddi ar y cae - os
mai dim ond ei fod yn gwybod . Peidiwch â
newid buddy , y byd yn lle mwy diddorol !!

One of the nicest blokes in world rugby, and
one of the funniest off the field - if only he knew.

Don't change buddy, the worlds a more
interesting place.

George North

Northampton Saints, Wales and British and Irish Lions.

....

Lendrid: *"I love all that text-speak. LOL,
WTF, KBA, OMG."*
George: *"What does KBA mean?"*
Lendrid: *"Can't Be Arsed."*

"I can easily get down to 9%. I'll simply shred my skin."

....

Lendrid in a restaurant: *"Urgh! I hate pizza so much."*
Waiter: *"Can I take your order please sir?"*
Lendrid: *"Erm, yes. I'll have pizza please."*

....

Me: *"I've never met a Thai woman before."*
Lendrid: *"I have. She was from China."*
Me: *"That's Chinese."*

George: *"I hear you're doing a session with Kyran Bracken every fortnight."*
Lendrid: *"I am, but not every fortnight. He's only up twice a month."*

....

"I can easily get down to 9%. I'll simply shred my skin."

....

"I can name Santa's reindeer. Rudolph, Prancer and Vincent."

....

Ben: *"Right I'm laying down my foot."*
Tom: *"Think you mean putting your foot down bud."*

Having roomed with Lenny for many years now, you certainly become accustomed to his very unique sense of humour and personality - with rarely a dull moment!

There have been so many memorable incidents it is hard to pick one, from him passing out in a weather spoons toilet as a fresh faced 18 year old, to his confusing quotes such as, *"we have to start what we have finished!"*

It really has been a pleasure being pals and look forward to many more years of friendship and comedy moments. Congrats on your wedding day, hope it all goes well - and am sure it will be a day you won't forget!

Matthew Smith

Leicester Tigers.

....

Maybe Ben will do a few book signings if he learns to spell his name in time.

Karl Pilkington 2015

INSIDE GEORGE CHUTER'S HEAD

Much like the clapping monkey inside Homer Simpsons head, what goes on in George Chuter's head, creator of @stuffbensaid, is as much a mystery as to where Ben gets his train of thought from.

But this chapter pays homage to these two geniuses and their love of film and historical figures.

I give you @stuffbensaid, thoughts through the ages...

··

"We shall go on to the end, we shall fight in France, we shall fight on the seas and oceans, we shall fight with growing confidence and growing strength in the air, we shall defend our island, whatever the cost maybe, we shall fight on the beaches, we shall fight on the landing grounds, we shall fight in the fields and in the streets, we shall fight in the hills; we shall never surrender, and even if, which I do not for a moment believe, this island or a large part of it were subjugated and starving, then our empire beyond the seas, armed and guarded by the British fleet, would carry on the struggle, until, in God's good time, the new world, with all its power and might, steps forth to the rescue and the liberation of the old.

But, before we do that, we will read @stuffbensaid. Never, in the field of human comedy, has so much laughter amused so many people, without the comedian knowing it."

Winston Churchill

....

"I have a dream that one day this nation will rise up and live out the true meaning of @stuffbensaid." We hold these truths to be self-evident that all men are created equal. But some men are created more equal than others. One of those men is Lendrid. I have a dream, that one day; we will not judge Lenny by the colour of his skin, but by the stupidity that comes out of his mouth. That day, we will all be free."

Dr. Martin Luther King

....

"Today, in the world of freedom, the proudest boast is Ich bin ein Lendrider. (I am a Lendrid fan)"

John F. Kennedy

"Once more unto the breach, dear friends,
once more; Or close the wall up with our
English dead. In peace there's nothing so becomes a
man. As modest stillness and humility:
But when the blast of war blows in our ears,
Then imitate the action of the tiger;
Stiffen the sinews, summon up the blood,
Disguise fair nature with hard-favoured rage;
And pick up your copies of @stuffbensaid!"

King Henry V

....

"In the Universe, it may be that primitive life is
very common and intelligent life is fairly rare.
Some would say intelligent life has yet to occur
on Earth. I think this book confirms that.
Congratulations Lendrid."

Stephen Hawkings (Genius)

....

"Lendrid, if brains were gold you'd be poorer than
Weasley - and that's saying something."

J.K.Rowling

"Well, you look nervous. Is it the scars? You wanna know how I got 'em? So I had a wife, beautiful, like you, who tells me I worry too much. Who tells me I oughta smile more. Who gambles and gets in deep with the sharks. One day, they carve her face, and we have no money for surgeries. She can't take it. I just want to see her smile again, hmm? I just want her to know that I don't care about the scars. So, I read a copy of @stuffbensaid and do this to myself. And you know what? She can't stand the sight of me! She leaves. Now I see the funny side. Now I'm always smiling!"

The Joker - 'The Dark Knight'

....

"I'd like to say something that I've prepared tonight.

Hello. How 'bout that ride in? I guess that's why they call it Sin City. You guys might not know this, but I consider myself a bit of a loner. I tend to think of myself as a one-man wolf pack. But when my sister brought Lendrid home, I knew he was one of my own. And my wolf pack, it grew by one.

So - there were two of us in the wolf pack. I was alone first in the pack, and then Lendrid joined in later, and six months ago, when Lendrid introduced me to you guys, I thought, 'Wait a second, could it be?' And now I know for sure, I just added two more guys to my wolf pack. Four of us wolves, running around the desert together, in Las Vegas, looking for strippers and cocaine. So tonight, I make a toast! Blood brothers!"

Alan Garner - 'The Hangover'

....

"Aye, fight and you may die. Run and you'll live - at least a while. And dying in your beds many years from now, would you be willing to trade all the days from this day to that for one chance, just one chance to come back here and tell our enemies that they may take our lives, but they'll never take our copy of @stuffbensaid!!"

William Wallace - 'Braveheart'

....

"THIS IS @STUFFBENSAID!!!!"

King Leonidas - '300'

"My name is Maximus Decimus Meridius. Father to a murdered son. Husband to a murdered wife. Wine snob. Rugby league addict. Lover of @stuffbensaid, and living life with no regrets."#YOLO

Maximus Decimus Meridius - 'Gladiator'

Commander of the armies of the North, General of the Felix Legions, loyal servant to the true emperor, Marcus Aurelius.

....

"Sons of Gondor, of Rohan. My brothers. I see in your eyes the same fear that would take the heart of me!

A day may come, when the courage of men fails, when we forsake our friends and break all bonds of fellowship, but it is not this day!

An hour of wolves and shattered shields when the age of men comes crashing down.

But it is not this day! This day we fight!

By all that you hold dear on this good earth, I bid you, stand, men of the West!

READ @stuffbensaid!!"

Aragorn - 'Lord of the Rings'

"Lendrid and @stuffbensaid are awesome. Fact! Triple stamp, no erasies, touch blue make it true."

Lloyd Christmas - 'Dumb & Dumber'

....

"Just when I thought Lendrid couldn't possibly be any dumber, he goes and does something like this... and totally redeems himself!"

Harry Dunne - 'Dumb & Dumber'

....

"May the Farce be with you."

Luke Skywalker - 'Star Wars'